Purpose
& DEVIL PISS

ROBERT SIEK

SIBLING RIVALRY PRESS
LITTLE ROCK, ARKANSAS
WWW.SIBLINGRIVALRYPRESS.COM

Purpose and Devil Piss

Copyright © 2013, 2015 by Robert Siek

Cover photo courtesy of the author

Author photo: Ryan Collier

Cover design by Mona Z. Kraculdy

Sibling Rivalry Press, LLC
PO Box 26147
Little Rock, AR 72221

info@siblingrivalrypress.com

www.siblingrivalrypress.com

ISBN: 978-1-937420-50-5

Library of Congress Control Number: 2013945841

First Sibling Rivalry Press Edition, October 2013
Second Sibling Rivalry Press Edition, May 2015

TO RYAN

Contents

Purpose

& DEVIL PISS

BEGIN

1979

Ten rows away from the back of the movie theater,
1979, my Dad and I watch *The Brood*. Mutant-face midgets
climb a kindergarten teacher, attack her with toy hammers,
other colorful weapons. One figure hangs from her shoulders
dressed in a down winter jacket. Its hood worn up.
Her face enlarged onscreen—even lipstick, Hollywood scream—
and blood spots are flicked like wet confetti. The teacher collapses.
Students stand watching. Red stains grow through her blue cotton dress;
small arms drum the life out of her, and maybe she was wearing
a brown wool blazer. I was five at the time.
The shot switches to her dead face,
and the mini-monsters leave with the main character's daughter.
I peer over the back of my seat, trying to see swinging doors
or the farthest back wall. Shapes are moving in the last row,
like ink spots on Rorschach tests—three dimensional, animated—
as though breathing under sheets like inflated body bags
filled with morgue storage, victims in horror movies.
I'm next to my father, so I worry for both of us.
This is the second time I witness this—the first during *Phantasm*,
the plot led to a funeral home, yellow blood squirting from a hand
following dismembered fingers and floating spheres of surgical steel
drilling into people's heads. I looked to my right every two minutes
wondering when to duck. Headlights hit the windshield,
creating shadows on the dash. I'm alone in my father's work van
sitting on a folded blanket in the back surrounded by auto glass
in racks and some bins filled with sealants, razors, and gloves.
It's early evening in the racetrack parking lot. Dad told me
to keep the doors locked. Our dog Baron sits in the passenger seat:
pony-sized with wiry brown and black hair, an Airdale terrier
standing guard while Dad is gone. Another set of headlights flash inside,
and Baron watches something go by. I hear cars drive. He said he'd be quick.
I wanted to pick horses, place bets. Lights invade again, like the moon
dropped feet from the roof of the van or a movie projector aimed overhead,
focusing on the rear doors, exposing airborne particles like flashlights in dark hallways
or torches in castle corridors, lighthouses on mainland shores, or search parties
in forests pre-dawn—parents urging everyone to keep looking, like horror movies
didn't exist and locked doors never really made a difference. An engine turns off,
no more floor lights in the aisles. I'm alone in a van, picturing creatures,

child-size and faceless, kidnapping kindergarteners, blackness above me, behind me—
ink stains bleeding on paper—like trapped in a body bag, inflated, breathing.
I crawl up front behind the driver's seat, hiding from nothing.
Baron looks down at me, panting and wagging.

Dreaming It

This kid claimed he could astral project,
enter my dreams while I slept;
he was jealous that I fingered his ex,
her pussy in the movie theater, watching
Rocky Horror. We always made out
at the same scene: Magenta and Columbia
singing, "I want to be dirty."
I should have worn Mickey Mouse ears,
pajamas; it would have been killer.
I could have played a character, done drag.
My friend Tim played Frankenfurter
and sat on my lap in panties
and fishnets. I liked it but pretended
not to, like seventh-grade boys in class
picturing warts on old-women faces
hoping to lose a hard-on before the bell rings.
That kid turned out to be a fag too. Last I heard,
he lives in Manhattan, begging for change on sidewalks,
somewhere on St. Mark's Place so he can buy heroin.
I bet he can't astral project anymore; I did see him
in a dream once, when I was seventeen and jerking off
to gay porn in an empty room in a strange house,
one hand chained to a radiator. I was naked,
and he watched from the doorway, sucking
his index finger. We never discussed it
or his ex-girlfriend's vagina or how
Tim's thighs were pale and hairy.
I'd place my hands on them
inside the movie theater,
watching *Rocky Horror*,
aware of my slight hard-on
like a junkie sitting on the sidewalk,
asking for help, claiming he'll do anything,
if you just give him some change.

Photo in the Silver Bedroom

Clubkids, late-night exhibitionists within this scene,
sitting center, oh so toxic, snorting powders assorted
from one hand or another. It's a New York City dance club,
the Tunnel on 27th Street. Steff and I pictured candid.
Eyes glance diagonal, divas recall it—in January.
Date burnt orange in broken dash numbers
located in the lower right-hand corner,
and we romped through a Friday at 3 a.m.
We, the broken mannequins propped in this cycle
of returning too often, collecting spider webs,
spending money, sitting, dancing, doing drugs till the morning.
Now, glazed by surprise for eternity in the silver bedroom,
a drug den of sorts and a background like large spray-painted tiles,
reflecting silver, stained purple, asylum-wall padding
like building blocks wrapped in aluminum, stacked uniform and all.
I, with black hair slicked severe, pulled with metal hair clip,
posed like a mannish woman or gender-bender mannequin
left out in the rain, eyeliner running down its face.
My Siamese twin, hair auburn, plastered worse with loose bangs,
matching eyes—one set blue, one set red—hoop in her nose
and my just-lit cigarette hung perfect, a Marlboro 100.
Steff's gray angora knit stretched over her chest
like piles of cobwebs tied together creating a sweater
and my black T-shirt too small like a growth spurt gone bad
with block-print orange letters ironed on from one underarm
to the other. This mid-torso message is half cut, yet legible.
It clearly reads, "PARTY," and we thought that was incredible.

Plastic Bags and Coated Leashes

I spilt safety pins on the dirty floor behind the counter at the drycleaners,
clumped like a pile of metal chicken bones, spread like broken robots
on a 2010 battlefield, and I pick them up one by one
as if they were individually touched by the hand of God.
This job tiring me, these moments boring me, it's amusing
to step on the pedal that makes the conveyer belt spin round.
I enjoy watching the hung clothing pass in plastic like a poltergeist parade
floating in circles. They move in a synthetic conga line, the human-length bags,
the wire hangers, the trapped scent of chemicals. I get off on sticking my head
in the machine when removing the clothes. I inhale like sniffing poppers
or a barrel-size bottle of rush, killing my brain cells ten at a time.
I can stand here for hours: the front door open, the back door open,
allowing wind to pass through, blowing little tags that read "Pre-spot,"
"Press Only," or "Special" up and spontaneous with the spin of an air current—
leaves falling, playing cards thrown upward, dust flying in balls from the ceiling fan.
My brown aluminum folding chair with my darker brown corduroy tie-on seat cushion
positioned so I face forward looking out at the parking lot, the walkway, at the passersby,
the rich townspeople, their Mercedes-Benzes, their baby strollers, their nannies
of varied minorities, the local animal hospital next door, and all of these people's pets:
their Labradors, their portable caged kittens, their boxed budgie birds, their children's
dying hamsters, gerbils, lizards, more dogs ranging from toy to terrier, from worker
to hunter, and their leashes, collars, pieces of material coated in an unnatural shine,
probably something to grip the lengths better and make life simpler and more boring.

Party Pooper

I miss three-day weekends (no holidays in March).
I think of a news-show study—why a second cup
of coffee can be fatal. I feel daring, so I have a fourth.
I recall my boyfriend biting my shoulder—
I enjoy rough but never tied—like driving slow enough
in a blizzard, or using too much KY. I attend a seminar—
how to use the Internet to order supplies—10 a.m.,
cafeteria, I'm the only male in a room full of women:
twenty-something admins, elderly executives, middle-aged
married ones, mothers, daughters. Mike from Purchasing
passing out packets, whispering, "Coffee and tea
on the side. There's coffee and tea on the side."
He slides into my row, arm waving toward me,
preparing to pass the papers like a relay-race partner.
"Pass it! Pass it!" I reach for the information and grab
like it's a baton. He says, "Hey guy." I thank him
in a deeper-than-usual tone of voice. I sit back reading
about passwords-to-be-changed upon first-time ordering.
I realize how I hate Mondays, holiday-less weekends,
the entire month of March. Mike didn't guide me
to the tea and coffee. He was too busy acting manly,
being a party pooper, acting silly. He probably
doesn't use KY, drives fast in the snow, knows how
to talk professional in social situations. He knows
where the coffee is, but I bet he doesn't know
about that killer second cup or that person next door,
my rough boyfriend, the beauty of individuality,
how to properly floss, where the wind goes,
the derivative of . . . the answer to . . . the difference.

The Battle of . . .

The temp knocks on the wall of my cubicle,
says, "Good morning," smiling like a troublemaker
sitting at the back of a classroom. I respond
while he's already moving out of sight,
gripping a Next Day Fed-Ex package—rushing.
I turn toward the pages in front of me, two-page spread,
an introduction to the Civil War, a timeline, presidential terms,
black-and-white photos of Lincoln, General Lee, battlegrounds.
I drop my red pencil—no coffee in the morning.
How do I cut caffeine from my diet?
I pick up the pencil like it's an oversized paperclip
and my desk is a magnet. I must have a steel plate
in the back of my head. Lincoln's face calls me,
the caption beneath it. President blah, blah. . . .
No "good morning" to the temp when I first came in.
I turned on my computer, then waited for the password prompt.
The day couldn't start till I typed seven letters lost in seven black dots.
It's all about the family of other pencils unsharpened, side-by-side,
drawn to the sharpener—electric, plugged in—like pedestrians
in Manhattan close to the buildings on a cold, gusty day.
I empty red shavings in my trashcan like disposing of ground fingertips
dried in the sun. I think of a coworker opening his umbrella outside
on a sunny day. He said his skin was sensitive. This was last night.
I notice that I dumped the shavings in the recyclables wastebasket—
switched again. *Those goddamn cleaning people—every day.*
I turn the page, and the temp walks by again. I hear his keys
jangle against his hips. I'm embarrassed to look up
like a Confederate soldier fleeing from the North.

Like Clockwork

My father calls my name up the staircase,
and I wake up at four in the morning,
like a door slammed or a glass broke—
my eyes opened—a robot switched on.
This isn't automatic; it's new, like combing
my hair in the opposite direction. He claims
that I have to drive him to the hospital.
His blood pressure is high. He woke up
drenched in sweat. These things scare him
since his heart attack seven weeks ago.
I sit up in bed, considering 9-1-1 because
an ambulance would pick him up instead.
I could sleep, then make it to work by 8:45.
He's not standing by the front door
when I look down the staircase, already dressed,
wearing what I wore out the night before.
I smell of cigarette smoke, and my hair
is sticking up like I participated in a one-night
stand. It's been years since I've gone home
with a stranger; it's been never that I drove
my father to a hospital in the middle of the night.
I brush my teeth. He's downstairs in the bathroom.
I can hear water running. I think of times I've held
an ear against another person's chest, that muffled
sound of pumping, blood moving, like the house
is alive. I put shoes on, meet him in the living
room. He looks stiff from anxiety tightening him
like a malfunctioning cyborg, like bionic men
were a bad idea. I shut the lights. He turns off
the television. We walk to my car in the cold.

Fresh Air

Something cozy about the smell in the room
like a stack of old library books pushed over.
The aged breeze is already dead.
I guess the heat is causing it,
transforming my IKEA birch-wood bookcase
into a six-tier potpourri holder like the baskets
on my aunt's bathroom vanity. The blinds
are moving like a flapping flag or a pleated skirt
hovering over hips, dancing on my balcony.
I've left the sliding door open to let air in.
My apartment is cooking even with the ceiling fan,
and the air conditioner my brother gave me
is still unplugged and on the floor.
Another whiff of moist pages, wet newspapers,
I look at the bottom shelf while sitting at my desk.
I stare at the book my boyfriend bought me—
an anthology, including three CDs
of past poets reading (heroes like Walt,
Ms. Sexton, Sylvia, and O'Hara). I made him listen
to Whitman's "America." He watched me
stand still, smiling over each spoken word,
sighing when the father of free verse
finished his reading. I picture my boyfriend
working behind the bar on this early evening,
Memorial Day observed, and wish he was here,
so we could play Plath's "Daddy" over and over,
laughing at the emphasis she puts on the word *bastard*.
I look away from the bookcase, stare down my spiral staircase,
and breathe out when a strong breeze blows in from behind.
The blinds clap like an audience or excited fans
watching a basketball game at a restaurant bar.
No scent this time, just a sensation up my neck.
I recall that cliché "something new in the air"
and laugh over using it in a poem.

Good Wording and Perfect Punctuation

I imagine throwing my dictionary out the window.
Perhaps it would land on the torn couch that sits,
rained upon night after night, on my landlord's lawn
like a homeless man hiding under a cardboard box,
ruining morning walks for dog walkers everywhere.
I've taken to aggressive online dating tactics
and lost hope for good wording and perfect punctuation.
I read headlines above photographs, men seeking men
on website personals like periodical searches at the library.
I haven't done a research paper in years, but I recall typing
in a topic and hitting Enter on the keyboard, like Internet
matchmaking, just enter your ZIP Code, the age range, and sex.
"I need a boyfriend." "Seeking Mr. Right." "Look, you made me smile."
Maybe he can make me smile, or maybe he and I will write love poems
or letters or see *The Color Purple* for the tenth time together.
Six different guys listed it as a favorite movie. One chose the book
as his best read ever. Like a homeless man balling pages
from a shredded dictionary and chucking them like basketballs
into a fire-pit garbage can, I continue to survive, to seek love.
I forget an ex-boyfriend, a bad dream—an SUV
making a U-turn in the middle of a state highway—
you smash into the side and explode.
I'm chatting with David again. He's always online,
early evening, late at night, whenever I check my e-mail.
He tells me he wants to treat me to dinner at a restaurant
an hour drive away. I've never met him in person.
We discuss body piercings. He claims most men
won't bottom for him. His cock is pierced—two hoops,
a Prince Albert. He e-mails a photograph—one shot of it all,
his hand, his balls. I type, "lovely," and he comments on my photo.
"Is it my dyed red hair?" He says, "No, it's your hot look."
Every word is important, and correct usage of punctuation
counts for something. That's what a well-known poet told me.
I drop my dictionary off the balcony. It nearly hits my landlord.
He's lying out back on that torn-up couch, arms crisscrossed
behind his head, looking like a homeless man. David says
he'd like to fuck me because I told him he could, and I'm obsessed
with online personals, the possibility of a first date and fingers in my mouth.

No Standing

Like a helium-filled balloon bouncing in the backseat of the car,
a soft three-dimensional mirror flashing "Happy Birthday"
every time it spins, I float weightless behind the wheel,
parked somewhere on 12th Street, his lips on mine.
His hands curve on my shoulders while my fingertips
connect to his hips, and I wonder when I've ever felt like this—
nearly five, wearing a life jacket, not moving in the center of a lake.
When I almost drowned once, I told Daddy I saw the fishies.
I rose to the surface through sunlight lighting a hole in the sky.
I look in his eyes, and my feet tingle when he says that he feels like a teenager.
Maybe I walked too many blocks and maybe I parked in a No Standing spot,
but the way I'm breathing is irregular, like pants from panicked lungs
exhaled from a body falling from a bridge seconds from the water.
I'm this excited, and he's laughing. He pulls away and then dives
back again, darting through me like a sponger shooting through the sea,
passing ecosystems, and touching the bottom. I shiver each time we separate,
and he says he should go now before wrapping his arm around me, pressing our lips
together. I inflate in the driver's seat like a Mylar balloon that reads, "Congratulations."
He cuts my string, and I float when he kisses me like I'm nearly drowning as a child
somewhere deep, watching fishies swim by. I want to fill a man-made lake,
climb a metal ladder, and do a round-off backhand spring off the diving board.
Like a bridge jumper committing suicide, I'll never catch my breath.

Leaf Blower

I question whether I was manic the other day
when I bought ninety dollars worth of CDs—
two collections of girl-group oldies and four new,
the kind you preview, wearing headphones,
rocking on heels at listening stations.
At least I didn't buy any box sets this time
or scan aisles of DVDs. I switch off the leaf blower.
Dad yells from the back door. I nearly trip on the extension cord
wrapping my ankle as I side-step down the hill. He tells me to get the leaves
piling behind the tree. I say, "Got it," and jump to the bottom. My nose runs
as I shiver like when I'd drive to a bowling alley, meet my dealer,
and buy coke or crack. I tighten my scarf on my neck
and walk in the house, grabbing a napkin to blow my nose with.
I recall blood clots filling tissues on Sunday afternoons when I'd wake
from alcohol comas or was it the pills? I laugh about popping
the date-rape drug before crawling into bed at six in the morning.
People feared those aspirin look-a-likes while Ian and I swallowed
two at restaurants while downing our beers. I toss a balled wad
of clear snot in the trash and stare out the screen door,
noticing it's dark out before five and realizing it's almost December.
I picture me and my brother as teenagers raking, landscapers for hire,
like the foreign ones on our neighbors' front yards. I've met a lot of landscapers
since I've been in recovery. I wonder why that is and walk out on the deck,
glancing at the gas grill and counting how many family celebrations
were held here. I hold up five fingers and cringe over snap shots
of bouncing Nerf basketballs off the oak tree, the one we tied
a rope around to hang our wet laundry on like preparing for tight-wire practice
at the circus. I pick up the leaf blower and picture the Father's Day my dad unwrapped it.
I thought it was a good present then. I charged it because I had no money to spare.
I turn it on again, watching leaves play leapfrog over ivy patches, hang-gliding
over the rotting logs we never got rid of years before I quit using drugs,
after Ian died one summer and I told myself that the party was over
because I was sick of socks with holes in them
and copying my friends' new CDs on blank tapes
I found in my junk drawer. I laugh over a manic episode
and thank God I have the money to cover it.

Bandstand Boys, Football Players, and Greasers

part one

Dusting my cologne bottles, dropping my right shoulder
and raising the left to each beat of the Jelly Beans
singing "I Wanna Love Him So Bad," filling my head
with 1964, a decade before I was born, three girls
dancing in sync, wearing floral pattern dresses,
buns wrapped high, little hoop earrings, big smiles
covering their faces like a number one hit
was in the works. And I picture the boys
cheering them on like black-and-white
Bandstand, so American like Dick Clark
asking questions about the future and how bright
it is. They mash potato with clinking knees, sweating
beneath plaid chinos, neck ties flapping like dog tongues
licking carpets or kitties cleaning paws. Johnny's top button
pops off, and he loosens the knot. Jeanie flaps her dress harder
spying chest hairs peeking out of his undershirt at the indent
where his neck ends and the sternum begins. Someone
yells, "Come on baby!" and Ellie yells, "Let's do the twist!"
The dance floor rumbles like tectonic plates shifting
underground, teenage earthquake, hips bounce
like bumper cars banging and spinning,
like real car accidents, 360s on the highway.

Bandstand Boys, Football Players, and Greasers

part two

I spritz Gucci Envy in the air, sniffing
the masculine musk that creeps invisible
like post-scrimmage steam—hot showers
in a gym locker room. A high-school football team
is everywhere. I'm naked and seated. They shout
and slam helmets, opening locker doors, passing
padlocks and benches. Photos of seniors in uniforms
standing shoulder to shoulder flash and pop like flipped pages
in my mother's 1963 yearbook—aged pages that released scents
And I'm touching my hips. Jimmy and Larry undress next to me.
One bends over like stretching for calisthenics, toe touches
before a game, sliding his jock strap from waist to ankles.
I bend forward and watch the dark line
extending from the curve of his back,
dividing his ass where hair collects:
twisted grass growing from a crack in a driveway.
Odors hit like pollution, almost leaving me unconscious,
and Larry wipes his removed jersey over his bare chest,
saying, "good game," while scratching his ass.
He splashes some of his father's aftershave, palm to cheeks,
telling Jimmy how he snatched it, something from dad's medicine cabinet.
Natural body odor and artificial musk mount beneath my nostrils and hump.
I squeeze my hard-on thigh to thigh, bunching a towel over pubes and balls,
hiding it all and picture a male dog shove its snout between its legs,
grunting like a pair of raccoons mating behind trash cans.

Bandstand Boys, Football Players, and Greasers

part three

"Leader of the Pack" blasts from my boombox.
I place the cologne bottle back on the shelf,
listening to two Shangri-Las ask the third
about a new greaser boyfriend.
They sing and motorcycles rev;
I sit at my desk in a swivel chair.
I become a doctor in a high-school nurse's office.
Boys wearing leather jackets are led in,
dressed in white T-shirts and tight blue jeans.
The nurse pulls a curtain around us.
The young men form a line and face forward,
something military, ready to fight—unbuttoning,
unzipping, lifting their armor, waiting to be checked
for battle wounds, injuries, areas of infection.
Denim unwraps down hairy legs, dragging boxers
to the floor: fabric ovals rest like fetters over feet,
like prisoners of war, my hostages.
I glance from one end to the other, make mental notes
on adolescent stages. The most matured one at center
is five inches flaccid. I roll in, still seated,
and slip into his personal space, feeling heat,
lava raining over my head from a volcano erupting
on a tropical island. He hangs an arm's length from my face.
I grasp his scrotum, my fingers behind his set. Warmth pours molten
through my grip, over my arm like urine running down a leg in winter.
He twitches within my cold clutch, something expected from the medical,
and his pubes tickle my palm like palm trees shaking against the sky
when the ground becomes unsteady, the earth's crust unbalanced,
earthquakes and volcanoes destroying small towns,
like dance halls exploding with trumpets alerting, skirts flaring,
and hands clapping over the music, like shoulder pads digging through
freshly cut grass as boys dive for footballs fumbled near the 10-yard line,
or greasers smashing beer bottles on garbage cans in alleys.
Inside, cologne bottles sparkle on my desk,
and my girl-group CD spins to its end.
The Shangri-Las fade out like streaks on cleaned glass
or raccoon eyes staring as headlights flash past.

Good Morning America

I overhear the U.S. Secretary of Defense
discuss weapons in Iraq with a TV news journalist,
mumbling comments about soldiers stationed in Baghdad,
sounding like a heavy breather hiding in my wardrobe,
pinching his nipples and licking the doorknob
of the chain-locked door outside of my bathroom,
leading to the house connected to my apartment,
where televised voices mix with laughter,
soundtrack to a short film shot by a student,
montage of a beaten woman sitting in a hallway.
It's the landlord's wife on the other side
chatting loud and knotting telephone wires.
Scenes haunt me in front of the vanity
while I trim my pubes over a trash can.
I think about running late for work and wonder
if she's on the phone or drunk at nine in the morning
like five months previous when she drove up the highway
drinking a bottle of Southern Comfort.
She hit a curb in Allendale and told me all about it
while eating a peach and smoking a cigarette,
sharing that she's a recently relapsed alcoholic.
I told her I had been clean for three years. It seemed
necessary, like flushing the toilet after moving your bowels.
I place my scissors on the sink and listen to footsteps
banging up the next-door staircase. My landlord's voice
masks *Good Morning America*. The last news I catch
concerns Mr. Rogers, the longtime host of a children's program.
And I imagine the landlord's wife hanging up the telephone
because her husband is yelling like she's an untrained dog
peeing on the sofa. She gags on her words
like choking on water, when people say
that they drank wrong or it went down the wrong pipe.
It reminds me of tape recordings played backward.
I walk into my living room and turn on the television.
A news report flashes a Middle Eastern woman screaming;
a tank rolls by in the background. I question if war is needed,
sit on my couch naked, and notice the volume is high enough
to fill my head with weather reports, who won some basketball game.

I forget the peach-eating drunk defending the right to drive bombed.
The anchorman announces that it's a sad day in the neighborhood
because Mr. Rogers has died, and I picture his puppets
in the Land of Make Believe, watching his program as a child
on channel 13. He always smiled while changing his shoes.

Turkey on Saturday

Turkey dinner with my family on a Saturday afternoon
is unlike Thanksgiving but somehow better than midday Sunday pasta,
like graduating from kindergarten one day,
then standing in a college auditorium
on another, moving your tassel across your mortarboard.
My brother and sister-in-law were visiting Mom and Dad
with my two-month-old nephew. I hadn't seen the kid
in three weeks, so I showed up to see how big he was getting
like an investigator seeking evidence at a taped-off crime scene.
My mother shows me on-screen photographs,
claiming he looks like her as an infant. I look like my mother,
but the baby definitely resembles my brother, like reel-to-reel
home movie footage, pre-VHS, when he began walking,
wearing a mustard-colored turtleneck and plaid bellbottoms.
Children weren't spared the fashion of the '70s,
when it was simpler, before the age of information,
downloadable pop songs, stem cells being researched,
the Twin Towers collapsing in my head.
I decide that the baby has my sister-in-law's lips—
too full, unlike anyone on this side of the family.
Stuffed with turkey and mashed potatoes,
I play with my not-asleep nephew while he stares at my face,
lying in his rocker-seat and grabbing my fingers
like my father clenching a drumstick at the head of the table.
The baby doesn't know what to do with them and releases.
He smiles when I say his name like audio recordings in slow motion
between instances of blowing air from my closed lips, causing them
to shake like "brrr" sounds made while standing in snow
like frozen moments on winter mornings.
My brother videotapes this, and I picture an older cousin
at the age of ten lifting me in the air when I was an infant
on some mid-'70s Christmas day. I'm screaming in delight
but I hear nothing; 8-millimeter films are silent.
I recall childhood fears of Russia nuking the U.S.
when the arms race was at its height in the '80s.
My nephew was born on Christmas, 2002, and the rebuilding
of Ground Zero is scheduled to begin. Thank God for turkey dinners
on Saturday afternoons and new family members to care for—
proof that something happened here.

Plug Filter

I finish washing a dozen glasses.
A frozen dinner rotates in the microwave,
revolving like folded clay spinning on a potting wheel.
Piles of silverware in the sink reflect a lightbulb above me.
I pick up a fork, a butter knife, teaspoons, ten morning cups of coffee—
two workweeks down the drain. I imagine juggling steak knives, so circus act,
wearing a cone-shaped hat, a ruffled collar, shoes resembling inflated flippers
like the clown costume I wore in first grade.
I carry a photo of me as a child from Halloween, 1980:
one hand flipped out, the other swung back—
tongue pointing toward the camera.
Mom stapled red wool-like hair to the hat
hung like dreadlocks, pipe cleaners, stuffed caterpillars,
then smudged rouge on my cheeks, showing like mauve moons or clear Bingo chips,
finishing the disguise with Groucho glasses attached to a fake plastic nose.
I laugh two seconds, drop teaspoons in a pot full of water;
they sink in the man-made pond past chunks of food—
week's worth of meals. Faucet water empties into it,
sewage in a bay, polluting marine homes—local swimming holes.
I imagine a clown backstroking on the surface,
squirting water from his mouth like a chubby-child statue
in the center of a fountain. I pick up spoons and picture my mother
washing dishes when I was seven in the old house where I grew up—
the front steps behind me in that first-grade photo, the pre-Halloween-parade,
I marched at Columbus School. And the house went down in '87;
my parents sold it to contractors.
I saw it gutted, half-demolished,
a wet clay cylinder-shape smashed inward, still on a spinning wheel.
The microwave beeps three times. Water drains, pieces of past meals
collect in the plug filter like dead mackerel bouncing in sewage—toxic bays.
I drop the silverware again, staring at dust on my blinds.

Truly Phototropic

My fingernails appear synthetic under sunlight
like snippets of clear plastic forced into my fingertips.
I picture Tupperware on a kitchen counter checkered with holes
like a catcher's mitt for a live grenade, and he crawls across the bed,
making my notepad a raft on the ocean. He buries his face into my arm
like an angel hiding in a cloud. His green eyes reflect light, reminding me
of identical satellite photos of planet Earth, and I'm tempted
to tear off his shirt and toss the notepad on the floor.
He blinks, watches me write; one of his legs crosses
the top of my right thigh, creating pressure like the weight
of a collapsed ceiling, dumped beams and rafters lying in loose piles.
I imagine being buried alive like a pair of firemen surviving,
while fifth-floor tenants of a midtown high-rise pass out
in smoke-filled hallways, flames causing walls to buckle.
He sits up, reaching for the novel he's reading.
I keep pen to paper like sunshine is supporting me.
I'm plantlike by the window, reaching for something
like life on a fire escape, children giggling four flights down
on the sidewalk. They ride bicycles and toss baseballs, playing
like heaven is on Earth, somewhere in New York City.

Auto Shop Mixer

My finger joints stretch while lifting a car battery.
I bend my knees, carrying the weight from the trunk
of Mom's car like a mover lifting TV sets, recliner chairs,
side tables, popping veins in thick forearms like a character
out of bad gay porn. Blood rushes to my head, morphing
nerve impulses into cyclones of "oh my God"
uprooting all other thoughts, like hundreds
of Midwestern girls named Dorothy
being transported to Oz, a hundred Totos
hiding in baskets inside flying farmers' homes.
I consider dropping it, frightened of its heaviness,
of it hitting the ground, imagining its insides bursting out.
My dad is paying for a new battery in the Sears auto store.
The salesman requested that we retrieve the old one.
I questioned this trade-in while walking outside,
waving the car keys and the door locks remote,
recalling the facial features of a mechanic
who passed me on his way to the garage.
He walked like a hustler approaching a john.
His Latino thug expression, thick eyebrows, goatee,
and licked bottom lip signaled scenes of bathroom blowjobs,
glory holes, and slow-motion cum shots on blond muscle boy
faces. Stall doors swung open in my head as I unlocked the trunk,
visualizing that blue collar Adonis stroking it off, saying, "Oh my God,"
in a trying-to-catch-his-breath voice, that pre-ejaculation and post-orgasm
shout like a scream echoing through wind-swept bedrooms crashing
in unknown worlds, flattening wicked witches, spreading her
insides out. I'm shuffling stiff-legged toward the store,
barely holding on to a 50-pound car battery,
losing my grip with each step,
forgetting how my fingers work,
accepting the numbness of pain,
wishing I was in that garage instead,
paying for a white collar attitude, bent over,
chest on the engine under the propped up hood,
a hot Latino mechanic behind me, tearing off my clothes.

Natives

Like Livingstone on safari, crossing grasslands,
regions of Africa, I dodge stampedes, round street corners.
Commuters dash toward crosswalks—antelope from leopards.
Pressed suits charge shield-like over wheat-colored hillsides.
Livingstone offered natives Western life, Christian faith;
slave traders hunted them, mammals on land,
hiding behind trees beneath the canopy.
I skip past speed-walkers, marching like musket-carrying soldiers,
shoulder to shoulder, human walls, military uniforms.
A middle-aged businesswoman shifts her right shoulder pad.
A pair of new immigrant Latinas half-run
with long hair in ponytails, trying to make the day job,
forgetting after-hours cleaning in a closed office building.
I pass them on 8th Ave. They stop to buy coffee.
Pigeons eat restaurant leftovers vomited from garbage bags.
They circle like termites in half-rotted stumps.
My saddlebag swings out toward the passing crowd.
I concentrate on loafers almost kicking my heels
when a weight smacks the back of my head,
and I stomp my steps like instant roots
lassoed by unfocused faces, like Livingstone
cutting hanging plant-life, hearing Victoria Falls
in the distance. Passersby reappear as I turn;
I notice a homeless man standing in the intersection,
waving a soda bottle and wearing an animal-print poncho,
shouting out loud, "Come on motherfucker!" I think *Thank God
for plastic* and wonder what happened. He doesn't blink for seconds.
I think of *National Geographic*. I'm a zebra lost from my pack;
he's a hungry lion planning to attack. I scream, "Jesus Christ,"
then take a few steps back. I pull up my sleeve,
stare at my watch. I have five minutes to catch my bus.
I wonder what Livingstone did when natives attacked.
Did he flee, cringing beneath his full-lipped mustache?
Or did he offer soft-spoken words and nonthreatening hand gestures,
attempting to tame the wild, the uncivilized and unsheltered?

Killer's Morning

In thick, cotton knit argyle socks, I walk the hall on my toes,
avoiding unnecessary noise that might awaken my pet bird.
Despite 6 a.m. and a blue fleece blanket draped over his cage,
he still manages to realize that someone is moving out there,
like Jason Voorhees in a *Friday the 13th* film knowing the whereabouts
of his victims spread over a camp site or in a large house. My living room
transforms into Camp Crystal Lake, and I'm an '80s vixen who found a friend
with a slit throat in the closet of the cabin next door. You scream once
and then cover your mouth, seeing a man wearing a hockey mask
walk past the window carrying your boyfriend's bloody carcass
over his shoulder. You crouch low, whimpering like a child
trying to stop crying after his or her father said,
"I'll give you something to cry about." I make it to the kitchen
and decide to leave the light off, although it's still dark out
like Halloween morning. Autumn hours have started stealing the sun,
and you scan the walls and counters like searching for missing butcher knives
in Haddonfield, Illinois, where Michael Myers has returned
to find his other sister, played by Jamie Lee Curtis,
and kill her dead for once and for all. The *Halloween*
theme music loops in the silence, and you forget what you
were looking for. Michael, in his white rubber-face mask, is breathing
on the back of your head. It's like my pet bird, named Killer, screeching
in secret, a hawk in the apartment, waking my boyfriend at a too-early hour,
even for a weekday. I freeze by the refrigerator, one foot stepped out in front
of the other. I whisper over and over, "Please be quiet. Please be quiet,"
and I hear a hanging bird toy knock against cage bars.
No more green-cheeked conure commotion coming from his beak,
I replay my actions in my head, wondering how a miniature parrot
now controls my movements. I picture Pinhead from the *Hellraiser* series
standing next to the cage telling me how he wants to tear my soul apart
for all eternity while chains shoot out from nowhere hooking into my skin.
Pinhead praises the beauty of pain while the taut human fishing lines
start ripping my face, chest, arms, and legs. No more sound
from beneath the blanket, the bird is sleeping again.
I lift the Brita water pitcher from inside the fridge
and place it by the toaster while I feel shapes in the cabinet.
I slide an everyday glass from the bottom shelf, over the edge
and grasp it in my hand. Killer caws like a sonic weapon, like Freddy Krueger's

knifelike fingernails dragged slowly over metal. I drop the empty glass on the counter, and it explodes into pieces, spreading through the kitchen like souls bursting skyward from Freddy's chest, tearing through his red-and-green striped sweater and always killing him dead in the end.

Holiday Eye Exam

Earlier I had my eyes dilated by my new optometrist;
I didn't need sunglasses when I exited the office.
It's late December, nearing Christmas, and the sun is far from shining—
another common winter day. It's a diorama scene, a shoebox wallpapered inside
with blue-gray construction paper. Toothpicks colored with brown magic marker
are glued together in tree shapes stuck in fake sidewalks, spray-painted Styrofoam.
I see boulder-size glass-ball ornaments, a red holiday sculpture in front of a building.
It looks like a sci-fi pyramid, some temple for little green men. There's a bum
leaning on a wall, his jacket zipped over his head.
He looks like the headless homeless man of Rockefeller Center.
His image startles me a bit, like opening the hall closet when junk
falls from above—your insides spasm; there was no time to jump.
I'm surrounded by shoppers in the moment, out-of-towners
staring down street signs, tourists concentrating on subway maps
before descending. I squeeze between families invading the street corner
like Martians jamming flags in sidewalk cracks, planning to take over the planet.
I say, "Excuse me," over and over, standing in place behind one person.
I scream, "Move!" and the man turns, looking at me
like he's witnessed madness for the very first time,
like I'm a schizophrenic pushing a shopping cart down 42nd,
praising Satan or Jesus in between quotes from Modernist poets,
like I'm wearing a T-shirt that reads, "I fucked T. S. Eliot!"
So I flick my tongue like a New York demon, dancing pagan midblock,
hunting cheerful children, cursing out husbands with staring problems,
and wondering when shouting in public became banned in well-behaved circles.
Winter winds blow on my dilated eyes, now tearing and wetting my cheeks.
I suspect I appear to be tripping on acid, pupils dominating irises,
moons eclipsing suns. I must look like a maniac—some freak
who hates Christmas. I'm on my way home to wrap presents
for my parents like any son would with the holidays approaching.
My optometrist told me I'd be fine in five hours.
The sky is grayer, and a snowstorm is coming.

Fireworks

Despite lights on in my neighbor's window
one floor up and across from my bedroom,
I read mail in my underwear,
standing near my desk, credit card statement in hand.
I stretch my cotton boxer briefs like a fitted sheet on a mattress,
separating folds, allowing the elastic to grow on my thighs
like rubber bands pushed up forearms or condoms rolled over hard-ons.
My white undershirt fits too tight over ten pounds gained since I quit smoking.
I ignore my belly when it's covered, especially when lying down.
It's like a throw pillow under a comforter or laundry lumped
beneath a bedspread to fake out parents checking on teenagers,
like my best friend and I in seventh grade sneaking out at 1 a.m.
to shoot fireworks. We made fake bodies in the sofa bed
in case his mother woke up.
I see my neighbor through his kitchen window;
he's watching me while washing dishes.
I continue reading my charges listed for February
and scan the statement for my payment due date.
I hope he's noticing my black boxer briefs.
I only wear one brand because I know how they fit.
It's familiar like this neighbor, one floor up,
smoking a cigarette, standing in his bathtub;
I know where he is because I often see him shower—
his shampoo and rinse through a partially opened window.
I only see midchest to above his nose, but still it's exciting,
like unwrapping condoms or shooting rubber bands, like sneaking out
at 1 a.m. to play with bottle rockets. He's done washing dishes, staring
through my window. I imagine him in his underwear,
leaning on the kitchen counter, or naked from the waist down,
hands moving below the window sill.

Groceries and Goliath

I'm carrying three plastic bags full of groceries,
all bunched in one hand like multiple slings,
like weighed down with rocks prepared for Goliath.
I lift them like killed prey, trophies from my journey,
my seven blocks walked to Food Emporium.
I try to protect my goods, remove them
from others' paths down the sidewalk.
Times Square tourists don't care
about strangers' eggs and yogurt.
I notice a fifth person eyeing my luggage,
my homebound booty, analyzing the translucent white,
perhaps imagining plastic-wrapped heads inside, as though
severed from corpses, blood spots trailing behind my footsteps.
I picture my arm flying up, whipping groceries like David under attack,
covered by the enemy's shadow. I spin and split three faces
with canned soups and pickle jars, screaming like the first-car
roller-coaster passenger one second into the first drop.
I'm running toward a family, flinging, frenzied.
A head of lettuce shoots into 47th Street traffic.
I shake my head, laughing out loud. A sixth person
concentrates on my bagged contents, forgetting people
walking in front of her. People dodge one another
like customers pushing shopping carts through
supermarket aisles, and I think about which suitcase to use
for my upcoming vacation. My grocery bags twist
like chains on swings; a child spins on the loose end
in a leather-strap seat, hanging like dead weight
and waiting to be whipped like a rock at Goliath.
David killed him with one shot.
There are too many strangers on my block,
too many tourists dying to see it all,
unaware that some people actually live here,
carrying groceries and hating the world.

Hari-Kari Holiday

Twenty minutes ago I considered hari-kari in my kitchen.
It was a two-minute alternative to washing the dishes.
I scrubbed some steak knives after pots and pans.
My boyfriend made lasagna to feed us for days;
it's uncovered on the stovetop, two chunks removed.
His is thicker than my aunt's was every Christmas Eve
when kids had their own table in my grandparents' living room,
and my great-grandmother looked for the cat every half an hour
while my grandfather hid in the kitchen drinking Johnny Walker.
It was time to eat dinner, and some time later we could open presents.
I just turned the water off, leaving three mugs unwashed and filled
with soapy run-off. Everything drips in the dish rack
like some post-main-course scene, like holidays
in the early '80s when nobody owned a dishwasher.
I hear my boyfriend typing on his laptop and our parrot screeching
in his cage. I picture the angel on my grandparents' tree;
it resembled an underfed baby doll, the plastic kind
with eyelids that close or those that cry when you pull a cord.
These dolls always had blonde hair, sticking up like bed head,
like spread out pieces of ironed-flat curls,
like the Christmas-tree angel's salon disaster, her bleached
clown wig wild above her face. A candle blinked in each of her hands—
a pair of orange-yellow bulbs made to resemble flames.
Her white gown somehow still looked clean. I think they bought her
in 1963. Eleven months out of the year, she lived in a box
stored in a closet in the basement with old clothes and suitcases.
That's where the cat went when she ran down the stairs.
My great-grandmother often got up to look for her.
The cat's name was Ginger. She's been dead for more than ten years,
almost as long as my great-grandmother. I'm turning thirty in a few days,
and I considered hari-kari while doing the dishes. I don't know why;
it seemed like a good idea. I guess I'm just sick of running water,
of dirty pots and frying pans, of remembering dead relatives and old tree toppers—
Christmas angels surviving decades like lasagna recipes outlasting the living.

Mother's Day

Since our most recent visit to Florida, my parents discuss realty
too often. My father's face relaxes when he says he'd move there
in a second. His expression reminds me of him sitting alone
on my aunt and uncle's rear patio, staring at a manmade pond,
drinking his tea and eating toast. Breezes pass through the screen walls
and ceiling. He looks like a person with Alzheimer's recognizing a relative.
It's just the enthusiasm for lower property taxes, day-to-day warm weather,
money in the bank, 15 minutes to a beach. I cut a piece from my birthday cake,
the one purchased by my brother and sister-in-law at some buy-in-bulk store
with a great bakery. My mother threw a small party for me two nights earlier.
I had invited over some friends to celebrate my turning thirty,
and now on Mother's Day, we're eating cake again. I pass a piece
to my father and realize that I've been cutting the slices.
In the past, I made one cut, then abandoned the knife
like an accidental murder, screaming things
like, "What have I done!" Is this an awful case of foreshadowing?
Will I be cutting my nephew's ice-cream cake on his second birthday?
Maybe I'll dress as a clown, twist long balloons into animal shapes,
or wear a Santa costume on Christmas Eve while my parents
phone us from Florida, residing in North Palm Beach.
They'll miss their grandchild opening his presents.
My mother will open e-mails, find satisfaction in attached photographs,
regretting her departure from New Jersey like a prisoner on death row,
wishing he hadn't killed that family like a serial killer who now found God.
I cut smaller slices for my grandmother and sister-in-law.
My brother's father-in-law requests one even thinner.
I think, *Why eat any at all*, questioning my lack of health concerns.
I've been drug free for over four years, so extra icing on my plate
is like a good-boy reward, like a dog's milk bone, a ten-dollar bill
for every "A" on a report card. I sit down to eat my piece;
my mother says she could never move away from her grandchild.
My father remarks that he'll move to Florida by himself;
his face looks more like it did in the hospital, a few nights following
his first heart attack or like a prisoner being strapped to a gurney,
waiting for a lethal injection. My mother is smiling from
across the table. My nephew screams, "Balloons!"
and points toward the ceiling.

Coffee in Camelot

The coffee pot fills like funneled chemicals, leftovers from a lab,
classroom experiments, the kind I copyedit in science textbooks,
dripping faster than last drops shaken off over a urinal,
more like a constant leak from a bathtub faucet,
a fifth week of twisting handles as tight as possible.
The super tells me he's waiting for the parts he ordered.
I nod and walk away wondering how fancy the plumbing is,
if the valves consist of bone from heads of slaughtered unicorns
molded in small villages and cooled in lakes somewhere in Camelot.
I pull a Styrofoam cup from a tower-shaped stack, one cup inside another,
wrapped in plastic on the pantry counter. The coffeemaker hums
like a just-flushed toilet refilling, copper pipes vibrating
in hiding like half-hard erections moving inside briefs,
constrained between folds of too-tight denim, like worn valves shaking
behind bathroom-wall tiles. I rip sugar packets open, hoping a quarter-cup
more coffee might drain. I hear the sink turn on, the sounds of a coworker
rinsing something. It's Rod in a black stretch T-shirt, the kind with sleeves
that grip above biceps like foreskin pulled back during uncut cock worship,
red tips turning colors with each stroke of a hand. His tan arms move
with each scrub of his favorite mug. I picture him in a shower soaping up;
his skin shines through lather, suds on his ass, shaving cream sliding down
from his just-shaved bald head. I look inside my cup, and the water stops.
He doesn't dry before grabbing the handle of the not-full coffee pot
like clamps on a flask held over a Bunsen burner, tilting to a pour
but still catching the stream like a plumber removing a pipe
holding a bucket underneath. He looks up, smiles, and asks if he cut in;
if it bothered me that he took some before the pot was full. I confess
that I planned to do the same. He nods while bending over
and removes a carton of whole milk from the mini-refrigerator.
The coffeemaker is silent. It's 8:37 in the morning,
and I'm dying to dry hump his ass.

Nine-Inch Cock

Preteen girls in tube tops and stretch miniskirts that flare with ruffles,
walk like lingerie models on Percocet or seniors in heels after the prom
following a set of parents and speaking loud like cell-phone chatterers on buses.
I want to pass by, continue a quick pace on foot in the neighborhood.
Steff looks willing to take my lead and sweep past daddy's little porn stars,
overgrown princesses impersonating pop icons and just being thirteen.
I tell Steff that I never liked the common people, even in middle school.
She asks, "What are you talking about?" and I say, "Never mind,"
as we make big steps beyond the girls now giggling.
They watch the Naked Cowboy, a street performer, play guitar in Times Square.
His shoulder-length blond hair hangs from his hat, almost touching midback
of his shirtless torso. He wears a bikini that covers his ass cheeks
but exposes his worked-out thighs, a pair of bronze urns balanced on boots.
I wonder if he shaves them in the shower from knees to nuts or waxes off nature
from the outer ring of his asshole like a boy before puberty, unaware of crotch stubble
and how badly it itches, especially in summer. I imagine attacking him
like a sneak-up tag, screaming, "You're it!" appearing out of nowhere,
like a game of manhunt on a one-block radius—we'd all wear black
and hide behind parked cars and bushes. I'd like to grip rear waistband, hawk claws
on prairie dogs, and jerk up, two crane arms lifting, ripping his Lycra and flossing crack,
giving the Naked Cowboy the worst wedgie in the world. Or maybe I'd wink at Steff;
she'd slink into the crowd. Our half-nude prey poses for photographs with tourists,
middle-age sisters from San Jose wearing T-shirts that read,
"I Survived the Black Out of 2003." When he stands at ease, cowboy boots
a foot apart, Steff swings in underarm with an erect index finger, jabbing upward,
hard like an eight-year-old announcing, "Look! Over there!"
poking the cowboy's asshole through Speedo, yelling, "Oil check!"
like a homeless man hollering, "It's the end of the world!"
The preteen girls are way behind. I turn back, waiting for a light to change;
the set of parents make conversation with the cowboy and sisters. The girls whisper
like saying, "I wonder how big it is," or "Tell him you like his underwear."
I watch hawklike, creating my own dialogue, digging claws beneath tube tops
like new boobies were ground hogs. His thighs are discussed,
bronze urns on cowboy-boot pedestals in a corner in the Met—
an exhibit of artifacts, ancient civilizations, children playing tag,
hiding behind statues like lingerie models downing painkillers in a backstage closet.
Steff says, "Holy shit," and I ask, "What?" She claims a man walked past and said,
"nine-inch cock," like offering his tool for a hardcore fuck,

like pretty girls would shout back, "Give it to me," unzipping jeans,
wetting their panties. We stumble like crack hoes, repeating, "Nine-inch cock"
with every other footstep, imagining more responses to Steff's new boyfriend.
We become seventh-grade girls, hysteric over first kisses, cracking up
with tear-filled eyes, snot running down from our noses.

Cartoon Bears and Cotton Briefs

Following my hand wave and evening hello,
the doorman looks up from his latest drawing
like a grade-school doodler called on in a classroom
when a teacher asks a question about Mesopotamia,
the river-valley civilization between the Tigris and Euphrates.
I press the elevator button. A couple enters the lobby,
a red-head girl in her twenties and a blonde guy carrying a pizza.
I see his tightie-whitie waistband above his low-cut denim waistline.
I'm holding a roll of gift-wrap paper decorated with animated characters—
multiple pastel colored bears playing in clouds and tossing stars.
I stare at the numbers lighting up, signifying each floor from twelve to one.
The doorman mentions holes in the street out front, shooting steam
like Mount St. Helen close to blowing up. Con Ed is working on it.
I think it's been twenty years since that volcano last erupted.
I imagine lava in the sewers disintegrating rats and garbage,
or valves like truck tires leaking boiling hot water,
borderline launching half of 47th Street,
like mines set off beneath asphalt and traffic.
The elevator door opens, and I say, "Good night,"
following the pair inside. The girl asks which floor I want
to which I reply, "Five." She says she likes my wrapping paper.
Her boyfriend with the pizza just stares at the ceiling.
"I bought it at Rite Aid. There were more rolls in the card aisle."
She smiles, remembering bedspreads covered in cartoon bears,
her flannel nightgowns she wore as a child in the '80s.
And I picture my fingers undoing the button on his jeans,
feeling the warmth of his bulge through white cotton briefs
as I kneel below and press my face into it
like an ancient ritual not covered in history textbooks,
maybe child games in Babylonia, naked boys in the Hanging Gardens.
Crayon-colored bears fall from the sky while monster-truck tires
are shot past Hawaii. I need an accident in an elevator—
his smell on my nostrils and lips. The door starts to open.
I look away from his crotch. He continues to read
the top of the pizza box, and the girlfriend says, "good night,"
while playing with the curls in his hair.

On Being a Good Patient

Tartar really looks like flakes of plaster
when power-washed from beneath the gums.
I spit in the rinse bowl next to the dentist chair,
and the periodontist tells me I'm a good patient,
that the left side of my mouth looks perfect.
He's pleased with the work done during my last visit.
I swore I heard, "rinse for me, honey," but realized
he said "buddy." "Such a good patient," while injecting me
with novacaine. I want to tell him it was years of orthodontics,
but instead I stay mysterious like a secret slave boy dying for home,
a beating by his daddy or a fisting by skinheads while legs up in an attic.
I remember raised hands in grammar school, knowing the correct answer,
struggling to stretch fingers to ceiling and catch the teacher's attention
like a boy in his football uniform sitting on the sideline whispering,
"me, me," hoping coach might send him in so parents could cheer
when he caught the ball and crossed the field. It's about straight As
in every subject, like my brother always scoring touchdowns.
My parents screamed, "That kid is incredible!"
The periodontist scrapes my teeth as if redecorating
a living room, removing hardened gummy—the aftermath of wallpaper.
"Your gums will cease bleeding and become wafer-thin." My mother
told everyone I'm in Gifted and Talented. My father told
his motorcycle pals that I would be a doctor.
There's a plastic hook in my mouth, saliva pooling
around my molars, stopping me from swallowing like poppers
held beneath a slave boy's nose while hanging in a sling; a man's fist
and forearm pushed in too deep. They stop him from passing out, applying
more grease to his outsides like numbing gel rubbed on gums before a first step
of a dental procedure. I recall my hatred toward sports, seeing myself
with raised arms—a football approaching. I cover my face; it hits
the ground. My father yelled, "Stop being a sissy." My mom
said, "Be more like your brother." I heard a relative
tell my parents, "Thank God he's in Gifted and Talented."
Another baseball game, another wrestling match, I'm sitting
on bleachers and reading a comic book. Now I spit blood clots into
a rinse bowl, catching my drool inside of a bib. The periodontist purrs
the words *good patient* close to my face. It's all those years of orthodontics,
opening wide, dental chairs, my parents reading report cards,
simultaneously nodding their heads.

My Parents' Pills and Butter

Crumbs on the kitchen counter
shook off from the toaster—
a white, plastic thing incapable of cleaning up.
This is days of Mom's breakfast that Dad ignores.
The mess she makes and mice she feeds,
possible rodent parties feast on bread.
Two butter knives out, lying in the wreck,
still fresh with specked spread—
what's left of chunks melted under silverware
that Dad throws in the sink, but not this morning;
I'm watching the house and dog sitting,
visiting this home I once hoped I'd die in,
my second-floor drug den, two bedrooms and a bathroom;
it was perfect when my brother left, I'd close all the curtains,
snort lines off CD covers, cocaine, ketamine, maybe heroin.
A pharmacy bottle on its side, two pills lost
centimeters from family—
Mom's antidepressants, Dad's prescriptions in his office.
I recall stealing Xanax; they worked at killing edges,
softening all-nighters, when cigarettes were smoked
filled with coke, an hour after I couldn't blow my nose.
And crumbs now stick to my paper plate.
I wipe the counter, picking up the pill bottle,
returning lost children like supermarket reunions—
four-year-olds crying for mommy,
an adult drug addict in recovery, trying not to worry.
I choose rye over cinnamon raisin; the toaster is overused,
covered in past crumbs, a white, plastic thing unable to move,
the centerpiece to late-night festivals,
critters darting across counters.
I thought I'd die in this house
like an unwashed butter knife
attracting dust in the dark
or a parent watching television,
falling asleep sitting up.

Devil Dogs Perform

Bowls sticky with left-over milk—
cereal for dinner, the television turned on.
Uncle Don on-screen wearing a Latex glove,
tells a naked marine, "A hand is a hand son."

He films this, and others watch, sitting on towels
in unlit living rooms, circled by remotes and tissues,
and the scene is scanned forward to three 18-year-olds,
soldiers, tattoos of growling mongrels on upper arms;

"They call us Devil Dogs," one says. Uncle Don laughs.
"Show us those holes boys." Six legs over heads, stretches
in a gymnastics class, these boys on a king-size bed,
perhaps in Don's own home or a motel instead.

Close-ups of anuses, unicellular organisms,
covered in cilia, pink and still,
hiding between butt cheeks
like three colored micrographs

in a biology textbook, 20,000 times life-size;
the filmmaker jokes about toilet paper; one actor
complains his hole is cold. Another says he'll warm it up.
Knees balance above while lower backs curl, cushioned

on a peach comforter. Scan again, the guy with the moustache
climbing buglike nowhere, pushing his dick deeper in his friend.
Don says, "A hole is a hole boy." Face bouncing at a bed corner;
he's blushing while taking it—his wedding ring showing.

"This hurts," he says. The third marine jams it
in his mouth. "That'll keep your mind occupied;
it's a big cock for the first time." Hands grab shoulders,
like no good footing on the next step up; his whole weight drops

on his partner, this rock he tops. "What about that hole boy?"
He says, "It's tight," like the end of a marathon, the runner ready to fall—
"It's tight." This is a favorite instance, when a person out there shoots,
when Uncle Don yelps, "Fuck that virgin hole," and the boy says,

"I can't do this anymore." "Fine, fine, sport," like giving up
midrace, hands wave in universal stop gestures. His friend,
an insect clinging on, scurrying weightless on another human form,
jerking hips like unfinished dog business when a puppy humps toys—

red rockets exposed. Pull out and zoom in, last shot of a wet protist,
cover slip off, the microscope raised up. This is gymnastics class ending,
last stretch, three Devil Dogs fast forwarded to ejaculating on one another.
Someone at home says, "tight," crumpling a tissue.

Cereal bowls still sticky, ass imprints in towels.
Uncle Don says, "Thanks boys." T-shirts unfolded;
jeans pulled up. Someone hits Stop.
An apartment goes dark.

Chat Rooms

Sunrise on 17 North, I take the next U-turn and pass an overgrown motel,
individual rooms like bungalows, spaced wooden blocks dumped on a carpet,
a baby crawling toward them. My foot bounces on the brake,
slowing the whole thing. It's 5:52; I didn't sleep last night—
we discussed his fantasies at four in the morning.

Eight-year-old boys find magazines beneath a king-size bed.
They see a woman's legs spread, one foot in a high heel
extends from a man's shoulder like a mutant spear
pierced upward through his chest. He is naked,
and one boy stares at his ass.

I pull into the lot of Motor Lodge Inn, parking behind a set of rooms
like the ones across the highway. The sun is up now—white walls, white doors.
He's sitting in his pick-up truck—a new model. It looks recently washed.
Red letters spell *Hustler* on a cover; he typed that his girlfriend was away
for the weekend. He wants to try something different. I clicked Send:
"What do you want?"

His response appeared in a blue normal font: "I'll pay for a room."
Twenty minutes since I fled my parents' house—I'm nineteen;
I close the car door like exiting a nursery. My hands shake like walking away
from a head-on collision, fatalities included, like a woman rocking her dead newborn
in its basinet, screaming to her husband. He approaches me. I stand outside my car,
leaning against the trunk, dressed in jeans and an undershirt.

He says my name when in reaching distance.
I imagine I say yes and hand him a secret package
like a scene in a movie—it's black and white and the fog is noticeable.
My fingers twitch less because of his wavy hair—his twenty-eight-year-old lack
of grooming, a day of not shaving. He tells me to wait, and he heads toward the office.

His shoulders remind me of an oversized high-school senior when I was a freshman—
a linebacker on varsity with thicker forearms than the other players. He comes back
and says, "No vacancies." I tell him to get in my car. We sit inside,
undressed boys, grade-school kids surrounded by porn mags,
all open to spreads, no longer stacked in a box beneath a king-size bed.
Parents arrive home early. The boys hear a car park in the driveway.

Seconds pass before they grab underwear and T-shirts,
kicking magazines across the floor. My hand hooks his head,
lost in half-curls. We kiss for five minutes;
my hard-on rubs on the emergency-brake lever.
He breathes heavy when I let go,
saying he's never kissed a man like that before.

"Put your seat back." The crotch of his jeans moves like knuckles rising under blankets,
football players in bed—flashlights and nudie photos. Double-fisted, I yank it all down,
seeing his bare thighs, his erect cock bounces toward my mouth. One hand holds it,
palm on his pubes. My other hand plants between his feet, rooting through boxers
and denim, fingertips touching the car mat beneath. I swallow it all.

My hips bang against the gears shift. The car is in park;
I come in my pants still gripping him, lips moving top to bottom,
saliva and semen escape with each motion. His head falls back while I sit up,
shaking like forty minutes before, driving up 17 North to meet a stranger
from the Internet who said his girlfriend was away.

The Nonrecyclables

A monkey sound from a crowd of teenagers,
definitely male, unseen, a figure on the corner,
a friend surrounded, hanging by the deli, harassing maybe.
It's early evening, supper for somebody; kids live unscheduled
out of school. This is the neighborhood by the soccer field,
fenced in, supporting local teams, fathers, brothers,
squirrels when empty, hunting through grass,
sun hats on senior citizens pushing shopping carts of trash bags,
like foraging animals leaving front yards, lids off of garbage cans,
handfuls of recyclables, detergent bottles, rinsed-out pickle jars.
Now more like a hyena or an injured coyote, same throat,
he's after somebody, a girl in denim with wet-look body waves,
bad ass with bare skin below a cut-off top. Boys in a circle
in super-long T-shirts, gowns on hospital patients,
another one lost in the Alzheimer's ward. The staff keeps a cat
for company, offering comfort to the dying, the elderly.
Maybe the fag crossing the street, forgetting his bounce
at that moment, not in heels like some drag queen—
he's possibly just paranoid. These children don't scare him,
doing nothing in the neighborhood, impersonating rain forests,
grasslands, savannahs, not African but more South American.
The subways are so third-world he thinks, all that pushing
and shoving. An old Italian woman plopped in the seat
reserved for the unfortunate, the physically challenged,
she haunts it like the homeless, stinking up the last car.
Another animal call a block away, the soccer field shaded,
the high school has it covered, after hours, urban letdowns,
that man in business casual, thinking about his green button down,
brown flat-front pants. Pleats are so heterosexual, baggy lowride jeans
so ghetto. Gates left open as garbage pickers flee in aprons
or navy blue housekeeper uniforms, everyone is doing it—
aging. Nonrecyclables deteriorate inside black trash bags;
his job is to walk funny and live in fear. The teenagers
might want to shoot one another, maybe fuck instead.

Neighborhood

Springsteen in my office; my boyfriend didn't shut off the radio.
I avoid memories of blue jeans, the American flag.
"Born in the U.S.A." stops my thinking dead—
that other night walking home. I obsessed over my safety:
where to buy a can of mace. Astoria, Queens, is darker
than the quietest streets in Manhattan; maybe it's my neighborhood,
the lights out home after home, red-brick residencies, an occasional
smoker half-out an open window or standing on a balcony.
I picture an Italian living room, something in suburban New Jersey.
It's all so Son of Sam. Didn't he shoot people out late alone?
I know it's not the '70s. I wonder what this street looked like
when people watched *Dynasty*. That soccer field
by the subway stop might have been a park then,
but that public pool a block over must have been splashed in
when civil rights activists traveled abroad, north to south
and south to north. Three kids kicked a fourth boy
lying back-down on the sidewalk. They knocked him over again
when he tried to stand up; not one adult said a word when rushing by
at an early October dinnertime. El Niño will kick our ass this winter,
oh no, I mean summer, like love and all, that's how blackouts start,
like flooding during rainstorms or drowning New Orleans.
Maybe everyone should sing "Born in the U.S.A."
while marching in front of the White House or form a chorus
as if the alter ego of fifty eighth-graders on a D.C. class trip,
posing for a photo on the front lawn where a Japanese woman
holds a sign displaying A-bomb victims after World War II;
tourists view aftereffects of radiation poisoning in Nagasaki, Hiroshima.
This background is like a scene out of a nighttime drama, something on ABC
that lasts for an hour, lots of furs, cars, diamonds. This neighborhood
is known for being multicultural. I'd like to purchase a can of mace
and hide it in my backpack. I get scared walking home alone.

Joy and Peace This Season

Like telling a four-year-old not to pick his nose,
I blow on my keyboard, scatter weeks' worth of dust—
my attempt to clean up. Two nights I forgot to call
Raleigh and ask my aunt about my cousin—surgery,
removing that tumor, if chemo shrunk something,
what's left of his pelvic bone, killed what had to go.
He's twenty-three, or less, ten years between us;
I was twenty-eight when my first nephew was born.
My sister-in-law had a C-section, Christmas, 2000-what?
My cousin requested a tree with decorations.
His parents spent the holidays inside their son's apartment.
I sent them a card wishing joy and peace this season.
It was mailed to the house in Goldsboro, an hour away
but out there. I don't have my cousin's address
or telephone number. Like ordering a three-year-old
to say thank you for his presents the night before his birthday.
Staring at the big box, he's upset with more clothing.
I was asked to pray for a full recovery.
I'm having a spiritual moment, explaining copy-editing
and proofreading, what trade publishing is, why I left textbooks
to work in Manhattan. His turn: details of my baby cousin's living—
testing lead levels in water, working for the government
of North Carolina. My nephew loses at Candy Land.
That night he didn't need to win over and over.
I didn't let him cheat; he'll learn what's important.
My cousin: "It is what it is"; me: "I understand."
I should call my aunt on her cell phone,
that number my mom gave me two months ago
before this past Christmas when my nephew turned four.
I pulled his hand from his face. "Stop picking your nose."
He laughed before saying, "I know. I know."

Golden Age

Face followed by limbs, organ systems,
you know, a body, still breathing, walking;
someone is too close for ten or so street blocks.
Mailboxes are nailed down; the homeless spill, step too far.
I'm gliding under God's stilts and clogs like Midtown on high,
especially on lunch hours—sun-pummeled, dry—when iced coffee acts magic,
dead bunnies in top hats, silenced but free. No big straws on the counter,
I'll manage with an inch to suck from, cluttered between ice cubes, caffeine.
What's with wool worn in June or strangers not saying excuse me?
Oh right, it's New York City. She told me not everyone needs space,
pays attention to his or her surroundings. Cousin Diane commented
twenty years ago, "He's so Manhattan"—thirteen and in Jersey.
Don't we all dream of living here? Old Broadway stars
blab on television, a PBS documentary on the golden age
of the Great White Way, five girls in a one-bedroom,
people chat at the bar at Sardi's unable to afford the food.
Who asked you? I'm getting away from it—Times Square,
musical numbers in someone else's heart. I'll trash this shit
strip by strip: the breakdancers, knock-off purses, a pussy cat
that sits nice for change on a cardboard box—a bum feeds it,
dresses it in doll-size costumes. Coughs reach your cheek,
two dozen footfalls from revolving doors, ignore expressions,
imagine eyes lost inside holy robes, heavenly skirts,
the stare into the sun, turning into Gia played by Angelina
on a runway in a ball gown, wedding-cake frilly,
dope-fiending for heroin and how did I get here—another face
moving backward, a roller-skater reversing, digital remaster thing,
play it back again. Traffic covers inhales, exhales, thousands of steps.
I'm on top of her, walking faster and past. The light changes
in two seconds, and I've checked for stamps before dropping;
there's the homeless guy who lives here, midblock in a laundry bin.
I'll share my coffee today, melting ice cubes wet with sugar.
All sweat outside of Sardi's, say good-bye to the White Way,
the golden age, my office building straight ahead.
This magic trick goes nowhere. Dead again
in Midtown—fake it till the end.

She Posed After Christmas

He photographs a neighborhood cat
on the roof out back while I knock on the window
to keep her attention. He's using our new digital camera,
a super-zoom Fuji we bought together. Merry Christmas to us;
the holiday passed. We have cat food for our favorite. He'll feed her
later; we find her in the alley where the garbage cans are kept.
Her fur still looks matted with the sun on her side.
She's on the garage, staring off the edge.
Light arcs along her spine, a solar eclipse, an added curve.
This must be what the religious sing about in church,
glancing at Jesus on his cross, his solid face, his nailed spots,
while they reflect on sin, how to remove a hangnail,
new carpet in the den, stray cats pawing inside ripped bags,
or a dead gray one on a tree stump, half-covered by a blanket
like I saw the other morning. I thought it was frozen, eyes closed
tighter than sleep allows or causes; my insides bounced
together and apart like I suffered a chill or an ice cube
down my shirt. "It's dead," I yelled: such a cold winter
this year, not really, but at least then and the night before.
What a trio of photos he got out the back window.
Our favorite cat in the neighborhood watching us in our kitchen,
her yellow eyes somewhat prism looking, a flashlight in her skull—
three different directions: forward, diagonal, down.
She's leapt out of sight now, but we caught the sun
around her, parts blurred in the image, although new
and in nature. It's one of life's rewards,
what those next-door neighbors say
is sent to us by God.

Fit for Worship

Wife-beater tucked into light blue jeans,
worked-out arms raised, trimmed pits exposed,
I see the brown patches that match the head of hair.
Fingers move around in it, styling, primping.
His eyes focus but where is unclear.
Maybe the corners of stretched pecs,
smooth bulges like monster ass cheeks
drawn on mutant villains in comics,
a bodybuilder's a third out from a Speedo,
flexing the backside in a competition.
He dashes to his gym bag sitting on a bench,
pulls something from there while I hang my scarf
over my coat on a hook,
and another man is naked next to me,
drying his right thigh with a small towel.
The young guy faces the mirror again.
His torso is now covered in an orange sweatshirt.
He pulls, positions, turns around and stares
over his shoulder. I finish my combination,
open my lock, and agree that his rear is worth
the long glance to make sure it's still perfect,
hypnotic, a prize for all parties involved,
male or female, stranger climbing a staircase
or a few feet behind on a sidewalk. If only
I had arrived minutes sooner, caught him
digging out briefs, bare legs over the bench,
the Colossus of Rhodes straddling the harbor
in historically incorrect artwork, but half-naked
in a skirt-like toga and proud of the build
reserved for Grecian gods, Roman athletes.
We're in Astoria, the New York Sports Club.
He's returned to his bag, fully dressed.
The other man slips on a pair of underwear,
then reaches in his locker. I start my march
toward another workout, a half hour on a treadmill,
heading nowhere, like Hermes waiting for instructions,
a sculptor screaming "bigger," but today I follow denim,
light blue and stretched over superhero hips,
jeans leading me somewhere. I'm seeking

the tight ass inside them, either seated on my face,
drowned in the Aegean, or forming on my bottom
with each stomp of a sneaker as I head toward fitness,
long stares in mirrors. I've witnessed the worst
of it, so Narcissus, so sickening.

Wild Wild Life

Waiting for elevator doors to open,
to escape the gym, another workout,
me still puffing in wet underwear and T-shirt
like just finishing a dance routine, all *Flashdance*
in headband, leg warmers. I thought I'd scream
at twenty minutes, wiping my forehead
with a carpet-stiff towel, running on a treadmill
and watching a trainer sprint full-speed
in an empty exercise studio, past a wall lined with mirrors,
so Jane Fonda teaching aerobics, Richard Simmons surrounded
by middle-agers, and the TV on my machine not working;
ones hanging from the ceiling featured soap operas, ESPN—
men talking football, closed-captioned. The Talking Heads
played on my iPod, and "Road to Nowhere"
couldn't keep me from huffing—a toddler told to stay still,
sitting on a relative's lap and being read to. I mouthed, "I'm bored,"
to anyone who reads lips. It all ends after lifting weights,
pulling a bar to my chest for three sets,
switching to an alternate hold to work biceps,
staring at an intersection from the closest window,
people crossing, streetlights changing.
I used a contraption that mimics smashing cymbals
while facing a mirror. Two guys were bullshitting,
pointing in my direction, maybe at the clock;
someone started doing pull-ups quick like the air
was better above us in his sleeveless T-shirt and camouflage shorts.
A girl placed a water bottle close by, then did crunches, knees
to chest; she did one set then left. I wondered if she needed more.
And it's the elevator again now on the main floor,
me and two women, cell phones in use:
one is reading text messages; the other listens
for "hello." I let them exit first. The phone-caller knocks
into the message-checker when she tries to beat us both,
as though dashing from a subway car to the closest staircase,
and there might have been an apology, but I don't hear a thing,
still blasting the Talking Heads, repeating "Road to Nowhere,"
and waiting for "Wild Wild Life" to make it all go away.

The Filthiest Reminders

The last Post-it note is used—
no more lavender inch-wide reminders.
I'll steal another one from work, maybe buy a pack
from Staples. Show up in an aisle hungry like an addict,
this chick on that *Intervention* show, an episode available
free On Demand. She uses computer dust remover,
an inhalant you need to huff for a high—
instant death for some first-timers
according to a pop-up fact between scenes
of a curled-up mess sitting front seat behind the wheel,
sucking up chemicals and sharing stories of molestations,
self-mutilation, how she wishes her father hadn't left
during her childhood and how mother was never there.
I could buy a canister—give that lifestyle a shot like a previous
six-year jaunt, all garbage head in nightclubs, my old bedroom,
my parents' house, picking tobacco out of Marlboros,
dropping small mounds of cocaine inside them.
This is what it came to at five in the morning
when snorting became useless, lines ruined,
a cut straw dragged like finger-writing on a beach.
She speaks to a cameraperson in the passenger seat,
her voice rises like an unusual comedian, the type who alarms the audience
with partial screams, outlandish use of curse words, or maybe a character
in a B movie, late sixties, early seventies, a Warhol production,
better yet, John Waters—a fifty-something in bra and slip,
demanding eggs while stuck in a playpen in the living room
of a mobile home. Divine plays her daughter, the Filthiest Person Alive,
and she sucked cock on film and ate a bite of dog shit, chewing then grinning,
"How Much Is that Doggie in the Window" the only sound. I'd smoke
a few coke-filled cigarettes, worried over the odor
in case a parent came searching for the source—
me watching television, clouded inside a funny white fog
holding a half-smoked cigarette in one hand, a gallon-bottle
of vodka in the other, a CD cover on the bed, coated in powder
beneath my driver's license and a thimble-sized brown jar.
Police officers handcuffed the woman in her apartment;
she threatened to kill herself when animal control took her cats.
Her sister crouched in front of her face, cheek-down in the carpet,

arms pulled behind the back. I thought thank God I wasn't violent.
She finally agreed to go to rehab. I've been clean for nine years now.
Divine's character was most definitely the filthiest.
Tomorrow I'll go to Staples and buy more Post-it pads.
I need to write everything down.

Alternate Ending

I dry a pair of chopsticks sitting in the dish rack
and imagine stabbing a stranger with one, unlike the woman
on a park bench at the start of *The Happening*, a movie
by M. Night Shyamalan in which people start killing themselves
following a strong breeze, the grass and trees shaking
as nature intended. The main character, a science teacher,
convinced by a nursery owner it's the plants doing it,
sending out toxins, airborne defense chemicals,
that affect us humans, shutting down our reasoning,
allowing zookeepers to taunt lions with their limbs,
fathers lying in the path of industrial-size lawnmowers,
construction workers diving from partially-built skyscrapers,
no parachute, just death. That first scene: she slides
a metal chopstick from a bun on her head
then jams it in her throat at an angle,
an act quite extreme, not your typical suicide,
and this song is playing in my living room,
a transgender vocalist singing about "another world"—
lyrics most likely about the destruction of earth,
maybe the end of days, but I'm reading it as a person
saying goodbye, concerned over missing the birds and the wind,
not really ending life, but preparing for his or her last breath.
I believe the song is about an individual because who wants to join
a team, especially one that is losing, no one-for-all and all-for-one.
The other day I considered the consequences of passing out handguns
to neighborhood children and how quickly that would exterminate
a generation. I hear her moaning how she needs another world,
and I'm still not shocked by faceless characters hiding in a house
shooting preteens on the porch who were only seeking help.
We know what the director was doing. The special effects rocked.
The audience can watch a boy's head blown off. Say goodbye
to the birds, accept that kiss from the wind, been doing it so long.

Being There

I'll be a blow-up doll tied to a folding chair
in a grammar-school auditorium. A relative
can push my raised hand with a stick
so my nephew sees me waving in the audience
at his kindergarten graduation. This is how I'll function.
And this is called being there, perhaps even the best I can,
a skeleton hung on a front door in mid to late October.
Because something has to remain shiny, a silver coin
half over the edge of the top of a dining-room hutch;
chandelier lights catch it when you sit
in the chair closest to the window.
And that's called hope—you get it,
all end of the tunnel, that business
of living, not surviving. I guess I put the coin there,
in my sleep or years ago on drugs, sneaking through
my parents' living room, heading for the basement,
the bar downstairs. A bottle of liquor stolen from loved ones
is occasionally the answer. So I stick around, like the rest,
thinking about a new CD released next month,
the one I must hear to elevate emotions
until my surface stretches and hairs rise all I-just-felt-
the-dead-pass and you forget. Blink, watch walls
change color, neons, skies at sundown behind the TV set,
framed photos absorbed into your aesthetic movement;
that's when I'll confirm it, glad to be alive. My left thigh
will pop, and the phone will ring. I let it go to voice mail.
A finger whistles flat. The apartment door is locked.
I'm deflated on the couch, a done-with doll no one will fuck.
Now fold it up, place it in a cardboard box. Please hide me
under the bed. I'll scream when I'm ready to be present,
flapped out in a wind storm, the next family celebration,
a paper skeleton dancing on a breeze.

All the Life Forms

Locker doors missing, some hanging by one hinge,
roid rage perhaps, zits on a back, too strong for his own good,
a monster at the gym pulled hard like a Frankenstein hug,
schoolchildren squeezed until spines crack and blood vessels
turn connect-the-dots on faces; it's this underground scene,
more mainstream but in the dark for gym-joining first-timers.
And oh the pants dropped, somewhat whipped down
with the thrust of a stripper, the sit back, here it comes,
the quick removal of Velcro-held-on pants, like flapping
a sheet out of its folded tidy, Chinese yo-yos crisscrossing
in swarms. A stranger's hairy ass exposed; maybe gone
commando, or his underwear taken in a power swipe,
the fastest clothes changer on the East Coast. My eyes
find the tissue box by the mirror and built-in blow dryer.
I'm avoiding long stares at the bare bodies sprinkled in corners,
decorations dressing up the benches and fine-wood lockers,
occasional white towels worn wrap-around on big-thighed boys,
wooly mammoth trunks, these muscles shaped, built from earth.
Colors vary like ground levels at a dig—we found another artifact,
a pair of prehistoric mammal femurs; I'd like to pound the dirt
with them: all fours and shit, just look at the differences
in hair patterns, genetics. It's easy to dwell on bare feet
traveling this carpet, over wet spots where others dripped
exiting the shower stalls. Another big bang is useless—
multiple life forms breed right here, in their flesh
or under the scene, some secret world
more of them should discuss, boneheaded gods,
all naked or half-dressed taking too long.
They're alive all right, like the good doctor said.
I'm an amateur at this, holding my tweezers,
my sifting pan. Who tore the door off this locker?
I plan on using the one next to it to hang my coat
and sweater. I'm already dressed for the gym,
the quicker to get out of here. I avoid folding.
It's troubling to decide if I'm disgusted or horny.
I blow my nose before leaving—all human
and timeworn—Chinese yo-yos shake in my head.

Holiday

It's Martin Luther King Day.
Tomorrow Obama gets inaugurated.
Out before noon, I stomp slush.
Another storefront empty, aftermath of a robbery.
So goddamn wintry, no flakes this moment;
a third person avoided, not middle-aged but elderly.
Local trips jammed, folks fleeing, somehow
I continue, spy a poster-paper sign in a window;
"Never forgive, never forget," black-markered
in angular psycho handwriting.
Have I seen it before? Taped up seven years ago,
days after 9/11. And how many terrorists have read it?
I tell myself that's not the point.
Italian Americans smoke cigarettes
in front of the bakery. I attempt to count coffee cups;
learn how many actually purchased something.
A red form enlarges half a block from here,
an actor in a Disney-character costume, human height.
Reaching the intersection, it's a plush blood drop,
wide-eyed smiling face, legs in red sweatpants jog beneath.
Kids encircle the volunteer and peg it with snowballs.
It chases them around the church at the corner,
a banner hangs on the gate surrounding the rectory,
advertising a blood drive. I fear the drop might beg me
to donate. Nothing happens; probably a kid inside.
I notice the Nativity barn is barren, a bombed-open home.
Baby Jesus and company finally boxed.
Mid-January, they've disappeared.
I'm heading to the gym, considering the worst:
it's a new year, doomed—a bathtub full of blood.
I laugh over missing Jesus. Let's turn it all to wine,
get drunk on political promises, rename the day
"The Day I Died." I'll lead a procession
over snowed-on streets. The new president
will save us; let's pray for change.

St. Joseph's Lavender Azaleas

A broken-off mascara brush beside a wad of chewed gum
spotted on the sidewalk near the corner by a street sign.
Sights of preteens applying makeup haunt the crosswalk,
snapped bubbles and boys teasing. I walk across
the street and the light switches to green; not much traffic
before noon. An old woman holds a wrought iron gate
which guards some driveway; she's rubbing her knee
and sporting a black blazer. Her face, a sheet on a hospital bed,
pushed to the end by kicking feet. The occupant was removed;
the fabric lies loose appearing like pained expressions, reactions
to a heart attack, features clenched. No need to stop, an elderly man
stands behind her, gray hair slicked back wearing a navy sport jacket.
They must be pushing eighty, and he has to be her husband.
This isn't my business. Perhaps the couple is resting,
marathon runners wrapped in flags, water spilled
over their heads. They'll make it to the grocery store,
their front door, another three-to-four-block voyage
because living rooms get dusty, one too many TV programs.
A middle-age Latino pushes a shopping cart with each arm,
a delivery from the supermarket, his wheeled loads consist
of filled white plastic bags, the kind you keep to line
miniature wastepaper baskets or to commit
euthanasia squeezing the open end closed
around a loved one's neck while a final breath
is sucked in hard. Dump the trash, someone is begging
for an end. The man genuflects in front of the church,
all sign of the cross, in between two shopping carts.
I laugh to myself, admire the azaleas
encircling a Japanese maple, twenty feet past the entrance.
Jesus is his comfort. I'm going for a run, the desire
for nonstop motion, no need to turn around.
Adolescence lingers with full knowledge that it sucked.
Some boys mess with girls, ghosts in the neighborhood—
tweener litterbugs. Lysol-sprayed sheets washed and folded.
Elderly couples exist on sidewalks. Who hangs their jacket first?
Last rites in hospital rooms, eyes blinking before a TV set.
It's time to dust the furniture, kick dirt from shoes.
I continue, full of fear, a marathon of patience—
loads of lavender blooming in front of St. Joseph's.

Routine

"My body is a temple," I say.
Lips clamped while I lick my front teeth,
as though examining the pattern of plaque
following a night's sleep.
I'm a size thirty-two now; I'll have the tilapia
with crab meat. This is fine prose
full of line breaks, not publishable.
This afternoon, I work my legs.
I took garbage out today, even recyclables.
I can do my arms too. A day full of errands,
it's eighty-eight degrees—humid
and muggy, finally not raining.
One-triple-eight anonymous tips posters
hang from stop signs, business store fronts.
An FIT college student was raped,
murdered, in the building on the corner.
Her mother found her naked, covered
with a bedsheet, beaten, dead.
Someone broke their chain lock.
The news vans are gone,
like '80s crime dramas televised
after sitcoms. This block is not
twenty-first century, whatever
that means. I run half an hour
on a treadmill five times a week,
some days less, like twenty minutes.
I'm telling you a story,
but without an ending.
Don't put this in print.
You'll regret it—a lack of poetics.
My body is a temple, so I'll eat my words,
wipe my ass with typing paper.
I try on a pair of pants,
model in a mirror. I saw nothing
that night, just read a novel,
never looked out my bedroom window.
Exercise and fitness—a full-time job,
the kind that kills one's passion
(I'll fucking smother you with a pillow),

near dead, on life support.
I'll have green beans with my entrée,
oh, and a cup of French onion soup.
Screw eight hundred calories,
overflowing trash cans in the kitchen.
Goddamn it, I need an audience.
"Don't let me die like this."

Purpose and Devil Piss

One out of four straight men appear nervous around me,
limp-wristed and reading a novel on the subway.

Certain it's not imagined, my days support this education,
stronger with years clean, a clear head aided by antidepressants.

I turn pages, content with fiction, brief travels backward
to recent moments on an off-white comforter, naked, panting,

a hand rubbing while I rock in minor jerks, legs spread
past his back, the guy I've been seeing this past month.

I come on his chest, an event earned, my knuckles numb,
thanks to overstretched fingers, red with my full weight,

a driven grip on a knife handle, Sadie saying hi from a hallway.
He said it was hot. Three weekends laughed in his studio apartment.

I lean back, lift my ass from his hips; his bed is dirt beneath me.
I'm Adam just created, with purpose, desire, the rediscovery

of fulfillment, a garden of options, plant life to name,
classify in books and offer to the public—

this is called ecstasy and these are five senses.
Another page turned, I look up a second.

A stare breaks, some male face avoiding,
fearful, like an X was carved in my forehead.

I no longer fantasize or read, but wonder why a stranger
cares how I judge him, godlike and punishing, a menace

in close quarters. Fuck this subway car, the people that share it.
We all stink in here, original sin bottled and sprayed,

a small army of foreign men, not with it, cologne bathed.
And last night on a couch in a nightclub,

I relaxed, his fingertips just inside my cut-off shorts,
part of a Halloween costume, a look from 1980; my yellow briefs,

slightly showing, as we discussed the weekend, the mutual joy
in time spent together. He joked that he doesn't mind

being my rebound. I said he was the furthest thing from it,
my previous long-term relationship buried out back,

beneath a garden, fertile earth soaked in life, devil piss.
I catch one out of four watching this kind living it—

too much to think about. I'm a Manson girl in protest,
shaved head and on all fours, demanding freedom for Charlie,

Xs cut into foreheads. I'll crawl till kneecaps crack
and scream so loud enemies drop dead. I have to finish this book,

text someone back; I'm the first man on earth,
no worries, no past.

Home

Rental in a three-story building,
I'm gonna blast *The Wiz* soundtrack,
imagine I have doors, knobs.
Windows open, all options, cartwheels
past moving traffic. No one heeds stop signs.
It's a double-dog dare for a single gay man,
weekend nights searching Craigslist personal ads,
slide some oil to me, men seeking men,
only in the neighborhood. Color me danger,
the sex and excitement, what comes after
bed death in a long-term relationship,
no nude couple for too many years.
Time to suck multiple cocks, *ease on down the road*,
relearn, unlock. Because *you can't win, child*,
but you can hook up, late night,
following e-mails, pics of a hard-on, a face,
a rundown of likes, dislikes, hosting or traveling.
My buzzer doesn't work; so text or call
outside my home; I'll fetch you in seconds,
pull back my comforter. Yes I'm clean,
fingers, soap, scrubbed feet, no deodorant.
It's deep, armpits open game. *So tell me,*
what, what would I do if I could feel
your hand on the back of my head,
my knees bending as I squat between your legs.
You sit on the couch jerking for show.
Well I'm a mean, old lion, and the hunt is over,
his pants peeled from beneath buttocks, skin and fur
stretched and snapped from fresh carcass.
He likes his ass eaten, turning, raising it
and spread, all fours, exposing pink of insides,
the folds my tongue befriends. Road kill reanimated,
filling underwear, STOP signs run down, shove it farther,
it's a brand new day, an accident at every corner,
a bottle of lube, a condom unrolled.
Is this what feeling gets? Pre-cum on my belly;
some people stare out windows.
This is my new apartment in a three-story building,

The Wiz soundtrack closing from computer speakers.
He wants to come in my mouth. I ask him if it feels good,
the taste of used latex. He's going to shoot, and *home
is knowing, if you believe*. It's a rental, temporary.
I'm kneeling on a towel. I tell him I swallow,
and finish what I started.

Animal

On a white area rug, he maneuvers me off my knees,
yanks my shorts and underwear the length of my legs,
tossing them toward a hallway and turning me over.
His tanned hands guide my lower half—a butcher
flipping a side of steer. My hard-on smashes synthetic fibers;
he smacks my right ass cheek, then bends forward face first,
biting my thighs at the start of round, uphill, pale rear.
I consider screaming, "I am not an animal!," all elephant man
on-screen theatrics. Actor on stage, slurring dialogue,
performing the hell out of it—this part, this man
and his tongue. Fingers spread like separating the chest,
dig in for the grip, pull opposite directions. I hear him sniff,
breathing "I love it." Warm exhales die in my ass crack,
haunting licked, souls pause halfway through the living.
Can you smell the deceased? A pig-farm atmosphere, snorting
here and there. I'm facedown in a trough, stretching in feed
as the hungry heads for a last mouthful; he licks the walls,
escapes my wet surfaces, devouring my back in small bites,
kissing before caving in. Eight-point-five inches, the butcher's friend,
his weight on top, crosses an arm around my chest, yanking my hair
with the free hand. And not an animal moves, four-legged stride
against the current, flooded river, drowned livestock. Dolphins
and unicorns, sunlit oceans, my face on a white rug, seeing stars,
the impossible—angels exposing themselves. He nips
my left earlobe, the third time the hardest. We take it to the bedroom,
pushed onto a queen size, with fitted sheet only, not even pillows.
My arms raised, elbows slide along sateen, facedown again,
and the whole thing bounces with a torn open Magnum, lube
squirting, greasing the entry, all fours collapsing, slipping, sliding,
some beast manages and I'm opened with ease. Rainbows
and flying horses, hunter crushing prey, something mythical beneath;
I choke the fuck from it, ride imaginary waves, going to heaven,
my hands holding ankles beneath a white dress, flapping above me
and I see everything. Not an animal on top, fucking strong, nonstop.
A butcher's arm inside the steer, reaching deep
then pulling free. Ghosts of things far from human
invade the moment in our heads. The scent of death

from his armpits, a washed-out pig trough, a seizure in a bathtub,
the pleasure of a full belly, and it ends on my knees again, face up
beneath his eight-point-five inches, the Magnum snapped off,
warmth shot from a slit neck, the insides of an animal drip
eyebrow to lip. I come on the sheet while licking the tip.

Haunted Homo

Gold Bond powder all over the bathroom,
dusting cologne bottles and the Q-tips container
in typical cut-outs from haunted-house furnishings,
dropped cocaine spread airborne on a triple sneeze.
This is late night and early morning, treating rashes,
a red raw groin area; it's time to fuck the dermatologist,
allow him fifteen minutes past the surface. He's one of us,
a cocksucker and proud of it in his white medical drag,
all clean-cut and effeminate wearing glasses and penny loafers.
He's seen the goods when I opened my robe—wine-colored
and out of a plastic bag—the tie fell off. I held it closed.
These things on paper, wrinkled beneath naked.
Legs folded, a secretary in a miniskirt, no drunk
celebrity exiting a front seat. Wishing upon
the brightest lamp, fastened to the wall,
attached to a crane. Please not bites,
bed bugs in the mattress, this city
under attack, these villains hidden
in clothing, couches, even computers.
Let Roscoe the Beagle sniff them out for you.
My fourth HIV test since March, tomorrow afternoon,
that load jerked out over my face, a phlegm-ball-sized
gob on my fresh chapped lip; ghost droppings drip clear,
ectoplasm licked quick or the second time that rough trade
tried to fuck bare, first messing, then entering, slid inside,
a wet centipede shot through a crack in wood paneling.
By candlelight I told him, "Just don't come in my ass."
A prescription for a cream with a steroid in it
and something else to eliminate jock itch,
a wicked case; he's suggesting powder
for hot days dampening underwear,
half-hour runs on treadmills, multiple squirts
of lube mixing with sweat, friction, loose muscles,
pubic stubble rug-burning my inner thighs, low hangers
smothering my spread crack, séances in the bedroom,
imagined invaders digesting life beneath clean sheets.
Gold Bond clouds when slapped in special places,
fog-forms fall like spirits crossing over, circles

of white on a black dirty towel, hard-to-see
swirls caught by the fan take off
past the window screen, the no's,
the yes's, the aging all over me.
Footprints in it,
just another faggot.

Bad Girl Gone Good

I do a shimmy in the elevator when I'm alone,
all Shug Avery in *The Color Purple*, shaking
that ass, shaking that ass. It's called getting stupid
when no one is watching. Maybe it's creativity
breaking out, or all common folk do this
when timing works. And possibly
it's love, L-O-V-E, thinking about
blond hair and blue eyes, the boyfriend
at home napping after a workday or mixing
beats on his computer. He fixed the leaking air
conditioner; we installed it tilting slightly downward
toward the inside of the apartment, aiming disaster
over my grandmother's sewing machine. No mechanic
wonder, just patient and clever, making me feel foolish
for overreacting. I finger snap with both hands, waving
them like pom-poms while thrusting my hips out,
impersonating Lulu from John Waters' *Polyester*,
the teenage daughter in red spandex pants
and tube top, blonde feathered hair—she dances
for the boys at school. I laugh alone and the doors
open; it's the twelfth floor, and this is a good mood,
the past six months, the spelled out and on the wall,
my success story, a match.com commercial,
his blond hair and blue eyes so not matchie matchie
with my near black and goldish brown, my high-strung
time to time, his almost too relaxed, the both of us
on antidepressants. So I shake my ass, all Shug singing
in a shack on the river, wearing feathers and heels,
very show-me-your-shimmy girl, dedicating a song
to Miss Celie, and this is most mornings
because the air conditioner isn't leaking
and the sewing machine is safe.
I'm acting stupid more often,
in my office with the door open
or walking to the cafeteria for a second
cup of coffee. Another moment slightly tilted
upward. Is this creativity exiting pores, sensitive
skin under tight clothes? I'm a teenage delinquent

on the TV screen, Lulu screaming, "Beer!"
and dancing for the boys. My boyfriend's got lyrics to go
with new beats. He'll play it for me later, and I'll wonder
how I got here, a bad girl gone good,
shimmying in an elevator, laughing out loud,
Miss Celie all smiles, Shug causing a scene.

Antony and the Bookcase

Wearing a black T-shirt on a treadmill running,
block-print word *crying* across my chest.
Bought it at a concert—Antony and the Johnsons—
a singer draped in ivory, circled by an orchestra,
band members at stage corners, my first time at the Apollo.
Songs about nature, the destruction of . . . *The Crying Light*,
the human plight; I'm running in place again, a loose book
on a library shelf during an earthquake like Satan is at it,
fork-tongued vibes through Earth's crust, tainting
literature, history, Christian fundamentalists. And singing lifts
and tumbles over heads in an audience, every emotion felt
by the well adjusted, the addicted, the entering a hospice,
the learning to walk again, the first time, and crying is not a bad thing.
So Christ on a cracker, an obscenely obese man struggling across
a gas-station parking lot; I watch through a gym window, thinking
this is why I come here—a place I've nicknamed the jail yard,
all cinder-block walls, rundown equipment, men working out
wearing jeans and construction boots. Muscles work when pushed,
undamaged, free of deformity. It's showtime at the Apollo,
time to get a full-length collection published, please the handful of people
who enjoy reading my poetry, attempt to battle the academic, conquering
voices: who's in, who's not. I'm crying for my word kept quiet, the weight
I work hard to keep off, songs about relationships ending, the temperature
changing, transgenders joining in camaraderie and love. Antony on stage,
tall in a dress, waves of fabric white and bleached in spotlights,
Lady Justice, blinded, emoting to a crowd of faceless forms
thrown from shelves, cracked ceiling, instruments played.
I'm cooling down, a Satanist in love with the sky, tree leaves,
obsessed with human interaction, a black T-shirt from a concert,
the word *crying* and attempts at climbing Empire State high,
a King Kong–sized homosexual to get to the choking point.
Scream until numb, a book cover missing pages, libraries burst
into flames, gas-station explosion when a car crashes pumps.
We all sit down: the crippled, the hopeful, the dumb.

END

Acknowledgments

I'd like to thank the following publications where some of the poems in this book have previously appeared: *Swallow Your Pride, The Rogue Scholars Collective, The Columbia Poetry Review, Lodestar Quarterly, Cat Breath: A Rogue Scholars Two-Headed Kitty Anthology, Unpleasant Event Schedule, Velvet Mafia, Court Green, Limp Wrist, Mary: A Literary Quarterly, Assaracus*, and *Chelsea Station*.

I'd also like to thank the following people for their encouragement, teachings, and general help and support throughout the years: Carol Stone, David Trinidad, Dennis Cooper, the New School Writing Program directors and teachers (1997–1999) Robert Polito, Jackson Taylor, Susan Wheeler, Cornelius Eady, Jason Shinder, and David Lehman, and anyone I ever had to sit through a writing workshop with.

Thank you to friends and family of course, especially my parents, Joseph and Joan Siek, and my much loved other half Ryan Collier.

Thank you to Seth Pennington, Associate Editor at Sibling Rivalry Press, for the kick-ass design and editing and all of the work put into this book.

I very much appreciate all of the enthusiasm I've been exposed to from Sibling Rivalry's publisher Bryan Borland, for my work and the work of others. He's truly a godsend to the world of gay and lesbian poetry.

About the Poet

Robert Siek is a poet who lives in Brooklyn and works as a production editor at a large publishing house in Manhattan. His poems have appeared in journals such as *The Columbia Poetry Review*, *Lodestar Quarterly*, *Court Green*, *Velvet Mafia*, *Mary*, *Assaracus*, and *Chelsea Station*. In 2002, the New School published his chapbook *Clubbed Kid*, and in 2007, he was included in the short fiction anthology *Userlands: New Fiction Writers from the Blogging Underground*. This is his first full-length collection of poetry.

About the Publisher

Founded in 2010, Sibling Rivalry Press is an independent publishing house based in Little Rock, Arkansas. Our mission is to publish work that disturbs and enraptures. We are proud to be the home to *Assaracus*, the world's only print journal of gay male poetry. Our titles have been honored by the American Library Association through inclusion on its annual "Over the Rainbow" list of recommended LGBT reading and by *Library Journal*, who named *Assaracus* as a best new magazine of 2011. While we champion our LGBTIQ authors and artists, we are an inclusive publishing house and welcome all authors, artists, and readers regardless of sexual orientation or identity.

www.siblingrivalrypress.com